SUPERNOVAS
of the
Heart

SUPERNOVAS
of the
Heart

BRENNA KATSOUDAS

Cover art by Elizabeth Whelan
Book design by Meradith Kill | The Troy Book Makers

Printed in the United States of America

The Troy Book Makers • Troy, New York • thetroybookmakers.com

To order additional copies of this title, contact your favorite local bookstore or visit www.shoptbmbooks.com

ISBN: 978-1-61468-535-7

DEDICATION

You always told me I would write a book someday, so here it is, for you Grandpa. You were always so sure I would do something amazing in my lifetime; thank you for thinking the world of me, always, Mom. Dad, Thank you for always believing in me to the fullest of your heart's extent no matter how crazy the idea. Zoe and Krista, the love I feel every time I think of you two brings me to tears. I am so thankful I have two hearts that make mine want to keep beating. Last but certainly not least, Bella. Thank you for being all of my red letter days and for loving me on my black ones. You have taught me the feeling of eternal freedom in our sacred friendship. I love you all to the moon and back, a million times, beyond words.

OPENING LETTER

I don't want recognition for the poems I write. I do not want people to bow at my feet, or compliment my ability to place words so perfectly together. I want to help you. The one with this book in their small, delicate hand. It has taken me far too long to allow this book to be released. It has taken me ages to force myself to let my pen rest and send these pages out into the world. And it is all because I cannot stop myself from feeling. I feel it all. Every emotion around the world, in every heart, all at once. As I write each poem that is worthy of your eyes I add it to the list. So the list goes on and on and the book never reveals itself. And it's all because I want to make sure each and everyone of you know how much better things get. And even though they are better, there is always darkness. So I write more, to teach you ways to cope with this said darkness. But the list keeps getting longer and the book never reaches you in time. Although I have thousands of more words bleeding out from my heart into my pen, read this with great acceptance now; The rest will find you later because this is not my only list.

> "…One day I took a long walk on the path behind me and I found myself along the way. It doesn't happen overnight. It takes a ton of long, painful, sad days and nights. Sometimes months on end. But one day you come back to yourself full circle. I once wrote a poem where I stated that, "The lost must find their way before they can love and appreciate the found. Once they discover their path they always return." I wrote that about someone I once knew. But now that I read it over I have come to the conclusion that I was lost and couldn't fully love and appreciate myself until I had found my path. And in these past few weeks that is exactly what I have done."

This is an excerpt from a letter I wrote to myself many months ago. I wanted to share it with you because it is very important to me that you understand the sun rises again each and everyday and the moon can keep you company on your loneliest nights. I searched high and low, cried oceans of tears and resurrected myself from the depths of my despair and I am now writing this to all of you as a promise. A promise that there is always hope, always a way out, and you will get better.

And no matter what happens, at the end of the day you always have yourself. If there is anyone in this world you need, it is you. You are far more powerful than you give yourself credit for. I sat around for a very long time waiting for things to change, and nothing did, until I forced myself to be the change. I hope these poems help you find your way if you are lost, but most of all I hope they give you the strength you need to carry on. Without the countless amounts of poetry I have read I wouldn't be where I am today. Their words helped save me, and all I can do is hope that by writing this book I am able to do so for at least just one of you. Discover your strength, be courageous, and use it to move mountains and set cities on fire. It is all within your heart, you just have to find it.

Welcome to my brain, my heart and my soul. Inside these pages you will experience my journey from beginning to end. From the explosion of my heart to the act of stitching all of the pieces back together. It all starts from within. And every night you lay in bed wondering why you're still here, and when it will get better, look up to the moon and he will tell the stars to shine their brightest for you, so that you can continue shining for us.

SUPERNOVA

A star that suddenly increases greatly in brightness because of a catastrophic explosion that ejects most of its mass.

Let these words create every kind of supernova your heart must endure to heal. Whether it be an explosion of great sadness or pure happiness, allow yourself to feel every atom that makes up your beating heart. You will shine regardless of the circumstances and the world won't dare to look away.

—You might as well go out with a bang—

TABLE OF CONTENTS

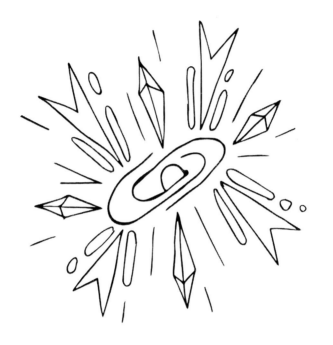

THE
Supernova

It occurs overtime

The thoughts circling in your head never reach
the half point of a doubt

you are so sure of yourself

and with that power you can do most anything

It isn't until something small occurs

a 1 on the richter scale to your tiny, little world

the smallest of lightning bolts strikes your heart

and under all of this unpredictable weather in the air

your enormous smile begins to shrink

and crack

With each shift of the tectonic plates

and each storm of rain

you reach the point of no return

It occurs overtime

The thoughts circling in your head stretch over the line of doubt

There is not a day that goes by where you do not
question every little thing you do

The power you once had long ago has been replaced with kryptonite

All of the small things that have occurred

now amount to much more than just the richter scale

continued...

SUPERNOVAS OF THE HEART

Your world has advanced beyond your control

The bolts no longer cause any pain to your soul

they have paralyzed you

The sun does not remember how to shine

even the rain refuses to fall from the sky

The muscles in your lovely, sorrowful face

fail to pull up the corners of your mouth any longer

none of this is your fault

you did not even see it coming

for as I said before

It happens overtime

—Paralyzed—

There is not one person I can pick out and blame

it's all of you

you've all had a part in this process of self destruction

but it's too late now

don't try to come back,

it's far too late

I've already gone up in flames

You'd almost think

you had been struck by an arrow

or a sword

but there is no wound to show

almost to be falsely mistaken with cardiac arrest

except your vitals are fine

because the wound is on the inside of your soul

The world seems to believe that

sticks and stones

kill more humans

than words do

And for some

that may be,

but for me

I would rather be beaten with sticks

and stones

and learn how to recover my brittle bones

than to have heard you say lovely words you didn't ever mean

and struggle to find a way to fix my heart

because

you gave me hope,

you played with my heart,

and tried to make a game out of this thing called love

But what you don't seem to realize, is that,

hope doesn't have a gift receipt attached to it

And my heart may have caution written all over it, but it is not a toy

And love isn't a game you play

it's something you learn to do, or you learn to live without

but this time it wasn't my choice, you made it yours

and now I have to learn to live
with meaningless words you've given me,

and how to live without you

I was willing to give you everything

but you didn't want it

Why would someone like you

who needed my love so bad

who needed love so bad

pass up someone like me

who almost gave up everything just to make that
breathtaking smile appear on your face

one last time

I thought long after you abandoned me

this would be over

but I seem to be wrong

because every night when I close my eyes

pictures of you flash through my mind

and in my dreams

you are everything I've ever wanted you to be

—*This is what has destroyed me*—

Hopefulness can create such beautiful visions

and destroy such happy hearts

No one ever stays long

come and go as you please,

that's what they do anyway

no matter how many times I beg them to stay

Some people will leave,

but never actually go

I search for your love in every passing face

Oh how disappointed I've become once it occurred to me

such love, no longer exists

If I wished to stop missing you would that mean
I would have to unlive our memories?

Because if that were the case

I'd rather mourn you forever.

Sometimes it is as soft as a warm blanket on freshly shaven legs

like it doesn't hurt at all

Sometimes it's like walking barefoot
on gravel rocks on a hot summer day

painful, but bearable

And some days I feel as if I have been shot in the chest

and left to bleed out all over the white carpet we laid together

Some days I can make myself believe it doesn't hurt

Some days I can mask the pain

But other days I can't turn on the radio

because I may hear a song that reminds me of you

And most nights I can't close my eyes

because you're all I ever see

I wish you would let me look around inside of you

let me see your mind

feel your heart

I wish I could give you all of the love you deserve

but I can't give all of my love away and have nothing left for myself,

because God knows you won't share any of yours with me

You're the only person who can make my heart so full

and so empty all at once

For the most peculiar reason

I like it,

in fact,

I crave it

and I can't stop

There has to be a reason for my constant return

but you must like it too

maybe you even crave it,

because you're always coming back

I have not written in so long

and when I tried

it was never good enough

but

once you came back, I gained the passion to write again

and that's when I realized I really needed you

It felt as if

my writing

had no structure

no meaning

no purpose

without you

So for months I settled

for the things I have written

but now that you're back

I promise

to only write beautiful poems

because those are your favorite

—*The lie I told myself once you returned*—

The vision of you being who I want,

who I need,

is someone you clearly are not

so please

if you want me to forget you,

I'm begging you

please

stop showing up in my dreams

Even when you spare me your time I can't help but think about

how soon from now you will give me not a moment

I begin to prepare myself for the next day you decide to go astray

holding onto hope for the next season you chose to remember me in

How lonely it is to be by your side

Is it wrong for me to love the way you don't bother with me

for days?

for weeks?

Is it wrong for me to miss you when you leave me stranded

without explanation?

without a call?

Is it wrong for me to long to be in your arms
when all you seem to do is push me away

further and further each day?

Everything about it is wrong,

but nothing has ever held this vision of being so right

Sometimes I want to read your mind so badly

Other times I remember there is a difference between what

I want you to be thinking

and what you're actually thinking

You do

or you don't

It's as simple as that

except I'm afraid to hear it

and you're afraid to say it

I care enough about you to rip my own heart
recklessly out of my chest,

isn't that enough?

It was dark

there was no way out

Not a window to be opened

not a door to be unlocked

In the midst of the night

no place for you to escape

As I was pounding on the walls outside

you refused to let me in

or maybe it was too dark you couldn't see the window above

or the door across the way

maybe you tried to

but the key didn't fit

maybe the glass wouldn't break

Or maybe you saw me

and you just didn't care

that

I kept trying to break down the wall to save you

until my hands bled

until I was left with nothing

I sunk into the ground like the rest of them

Another helpless breath melted into the disturbed

Absent from the only person I had ever truly known,

myself

All for the sole reason, that I

had given you the benefit of the doubt

BRENNA KATSOUDAS

Rain pours down flooding our small little town

Invading every space I saved for you in the walls of my heart

never realizing that maybe

just maybe

the water wouldn't have a way out

that you'd drown me

I bent over backwards and broke every part of me

just to keep the thought of you and I alive

all in the name of love and betrayal

He was lost and broken

His soul was unknown

Unidentified

He had done many things he wasn't proud of

witnessed things he wish he hadn't

Experienced countless traumatic deaths

cried too many tears,

enough to fill the oceans

Shame was his middle name

never able to look you in the eye

always at a constant war with himself

The man drank away the glorious pain

as voices taunted and teased

Realizing there was no more running,

no more hiding

Forcing himself to believe he was deserving of this

Punishment was his project

The ink told a horror story

That his lips could never speak

His fears

His blood

His tears

continued...

BRENNA KATSOUDAS

Everything beautifully, tragically, sketched in mud

Now set in cold hard stone

The machine gun sound

that drilled his skin

would never be as agonizing as the craters on his heart

He didn't have to speak of the terror

forever called his life

for the horrible story

had been etched onto his body

with sharp jagged lines, as cold as his pulverized heart

You decipher his damaged surface like a story book

feel the unbearable pain and sorrow

read the words unable to be spoken

He didn't want to forget,

not that he could

Tormented each night

Ashamed of his life

He wasn't credibly honored, but he was extremely capable

—*Glorious pain*—

One of the best things you can give someone

is hope

and one of the worst things you can do

is take it away

Watch the poetry spill from my veins
as he cuts me where it hurts most

Why do you do that? Why do you place hope in her delicate hands and just decide she doesn't deserve it anymore? How can you just walk in and wake up one day and walk right back out as if you were never there? You may like to think you never were, but she'll never be able to.

My heart aches through every vein and vessel it carries

because out of all of these years

I've never felt so far from you

but I've never been this close to you

—*We don't even exist in the same world anymore*—

If you weren't intending to stay

why did you ever return?

Betrayal

the best way to describe

how I had given you words I scribbled onto paper

believing you would cherish them as I did

only to find

they were all gone

just as you were

How could you?

Tears threatening to spill

all because I was stupid enough

to trust you again

and the worst part is that I don't regret it

not even a little

You will never forget the way you felt in that exact moment. From this point on your days will be consumed with comparing everything and everyone to what you thought you had, but did not, with him. It is the harsh reality of a one sided love. And because of this you will continue to look for him in every passing face. Right or wrong you still yearn for his presence. Although he is not going to return you still have a glint of hope. If he has taught you anything, it's that he is great at walking away whenever he pleases and damn good at waltzing back in as if nothing had ever happened, as if he was never gone.

—The revolving door—

We are told our entire lives

that words aren't painful

they're just words

but how come when they are spoken

they feel like knives in your chest

and gunshot wounds

to your heart?

How come I'm supposed to act like I didn't feel a thing

when the words left your tongue?

But I haven't decided what is worse,

the words said

or the ones that never had a chance to be spoken

She spent her life falling in love with things she could never have

Not to be confused with golden prongs
that held one of a kind diamonds

Only living breathing beings with beating broken hearts
and eyes that held the sky

It is so hard to continue your days
with a feeling of emptiness inside of you

It is even more difficult to understand why you feel this way,

when nothing had filled that space in the first place

Forgetting you never occurred

because

every time I heard your name

pain struck my heart

but I held in each wince

I could never let them know

how much I missed you

because that would get back to you

and I knew just how much you didn't miss me

Jealousy is detrimental

a sin

that I find myself in the midst of each and every time

the thought of you with someone else crosses my mind

The worst part is,

you aren't even mine

BRENNA KATSOUDAS

If I picked up a bottle of poison

and drank it without a thought tonight, knowing it was bad for me

Would you call me crazy?

Would you try and stop me?

Because every time I pick up the phone to call you

that's exactly what I'm doing

My heart aches in all different places because of so many faces

but you,

you are the reason it falters to a stop

the only one who gave back a little piece of what I handed you

and then out of the blue you stripped so many pieces of my heart

keeping them all to yourself

and you never had the decency to explain why,

you just left

I can't "just" go to the store anymore

It's not that simple

I can't "just" fall asleep

It's not that easy

I can drive my car past your house

but it will never be "just" a house

I can cross the days off on my calendar

but your birthday will never be "just" another day

And September and October will never be the same

because they have you and I written all over them

Under each leaf pile

every time the wind blows

I smell your scent all over me

suddenly choking on air when all I need is oxygen

because you're not here

but I still smell you

I still hear you

What a sad reality it is to know nothing in this world
will ever go back to the way it was

before I knew your name

continued...

I can't "just" look up at the stars anymore

I can't "just" write my poems about the moon

and the way you used to love me underneath it

I can't look at that stranger
and say he doesn't look like someone I know

because he does

he is you

I can't "just" hear your name

it's not "just" a name anymore

it's my heart

with all of our memories plastered across it

I will start and end each day for the rest of my life

praying

that it was "just" a dream

that soon enough you'll make your way back to me

I lay wide awake

and broken hearted

among this blanket of stars

that holds the key to what used to be our heart

How sweet is a girl

she only wants to love you with all that she is

How tragic is a boy

he only wants to use you

and then forget you even exist

When the smiles had fallen off of their faces

she had done everything to keep hers alive

and awake

Realizing that was not enough

she searched for more

picking their pieces up off the floor

Some were missing

actually, quite a few

so she tore off some of her own, and gave them to you

Nothing had changed,

the emotionless emotion only remained

Devastated at her failed attempt, she tried once more

this time ripping the heart from her very own chest

Stunned at her own actions

staring in disbelief

as you grabbed it from her hands

and gobbled it up, enjoying the feast

continued...

BRENNA KATSOUDAS

...continued

Though you still weren't satisfied with the ultimate sacrifice

Suffering from shock and a pain in her hollow chest
that will never suffice

Baffled at the fact that she just killed herself to save the life

of someone not capable of being grateful

to carry such a heart

Her last gesture was not a waste

for she lived and died without regret,

this was her fate

Her purpose was to give

and give

until she had absolutely nothing left

I did not fall down this rabbit hole

I have been pushed

by another version of myself,

I've gone mad

but I haven't tried the drugs

I don't even need them

My mind has driven me mad

all on it's very own

My body may be

but my mind is

never

asleep

It's okay.

No it's not.

And so it begins.

That was fun.

No it wasn't.

I like him.

Do you though?

I looked so pretty today.

Actually you're looking a little chubby, lay off the cookies.

I'm happy.

Remember that one time?

This feels right.

Well, it shouldn't.

I love my friends.

They don't love you nearly as much.

I like it here.

You'll never belong anywhere...disappear.

Exhausted.

This is a good movie.

Trigger.

continued...

...continued

I'm tired, I'm going to head to bed.

No you're not. I'm going to keep you awake for awhile.

Don't forget all of the bad things you've done.

You should stay up just incase you miss something.

Remember that thing that happened today? Overthink it.

Are you stressed yet?

Don't forget to shake in your sleep.

Goodnight.

—Daily phone calls with anxiety—

There is beauty in darkness

under each layer of destructive

is a glimpse into the light

Each day it grows a bit brighter than the last

Until night returns

and it is painted black and swallowed whole

Nobody on this earth loves her enough

The heart caged in her chest

wakes each morning

aching for the love it produces

and gives so freely to others

It never returns

One can only love themselves so much

until the misery

from the absence of love surfaces

reminding her

that not one heart beats for her

It's quite sad

to think that

when a star has burned too brightly

and has had enough

it will burn out

but the only ones who will notice are the stars closest to it

because that one stars light does not affect the entire sky,

kind of like us

If I died

my absence would only affect the ones closest to me

because my absence does not affect the entire world

In fact the world wouldn't have the slightest clue if I'd left or not

because I am not the type to create a supernova

I don't have the power to obtain the entire universes' attention

and oh how sad that truly is

Swallowed whole

by my own mind

Every second that I'm awake

Every hour that I'm breathing

Every moment that I live

and no matter how hard I fight

I can never win this war, It just never ends

Do you know what it feels like to fall?

And I don't mean in love

Soaring to your doom

from the highest platform

so far from yourself

This life appears to be an intangible object

in the hands of someone who destroyed you

You are that someone

Thoughts run wild

day and night

juggling your life in its hands

pushing your body to the edge

ultimately ripping your heart into shreds

and leaving nothing but the dust that has collected around your love

You don't sleep

but you do not stay awake either

Somewhere in between half alive and almost dead

sleepwalking through life

all the while knowing this is wrong

something is so terribly wrong

When I asked you if you knew what it felt like to fall

I didn't mean in the case of an accident

To be pushed intentionally to your death

by your own conscience

You did this

No physical pain

could amount to the emotional agony I feel

when disappearing

seems like the only option left

for a bothersome soul like me

I tried to feel yellow

I tried to remember I was yellow

I tried to remember you reminding me all I was, was yellow

but it wasn't enough this time

and neither was I

A gaping hole

in the center of your existence

where the lack of love lies

somewhere in which

your demons hide

Prying your eyes open at ungodly hours of the night,

rejecting the thought of an ounce of rest

Inviting your doubts with open arms,

giving grief a place to call home

as heartache burrows itself deep beneath the layers of your skin

penetrating your delicate soul

I have been the purest form of sunshine in every aspect. But as the evening sky begins to turn black, so does my soul. Because sometimes all I feel is happiness; and sometimes a dark spirit makes its way into my head and fills me completely. And sometimes all I feel is sorrow.

Standing between yes

and no

on a tightrope, with no net to catch me

The rope falters each way I go

The longer I stand in the middle

the weaker the rope becomes

but I like it

the feeling of not knowing if I'm playing it too safe

or not safe enough

Maybe I'll fall to my doom

who knows, I just might

After all, there is no one to catch me,

and lately I haven't been too good at saving myself

When people ask

I pretend I'm okay,

that I'm fine without you

You'd think I'd have it down by now

since all of this time has passed

but they aren't that naive,

in fact,

It's easier to convince myself

I sit here and write poems about being over you

I sit here and pretend to find someone new,

but the truth is I'll never be over you

It's not possible to stop loving you

It's been a year and everyday that passes
that used to consist of our conversations

is another day my heart spends in agony

because I never planned to lose you like this

They're all about you

They're always about you

There are just some things they don't understand

like how I fell in love with you in the first place

how your smile lit up my entire world

and all of its galaxies

There are just some things they can't comprehend

like how I let you return

even though you left without an explanation

or how I'm still willing to allow you to come back

even though this wasn't the first time

There are just some things I can't explain to them

like how there is not a single person I want more than you

even though I've cried myself to sleep for weeks because you left

and even though that song makes me
weep like no tomorrow, I just keep listening

because I miss you

I miss you so much that I've stopped talking to the moon

and I have done everything I can not to look up at the stars
because every time I do

I see your face in every constellation

It all hurts too much

and it's all your fault

but I still wish you'd come back

There are a lot of things I don't understand either

BRENNA KATSOUDAS

Every drop was an ocean

Every breath was a hurricane

Every cry was a crack of thunder

Every scream was a strike of lightning

You'd have thought a storm was brewing beneath her skin

She had created a mess of things through her own misery

Each night the cries became louder

and the storms raged harder

it was impossible not to feel her agony

Day and night

she fought for them

Until one February midnight the stars shown their brightest
and they whispered in her ear

"The lost must find their way before they can love and appreciate
the found. Once they discover their path, they always return."

The smallest of secrets in the galaxy

had cured the storm

and put a stitch in her torn heart

she never spoke of that night to a soul

for the secrets of the stars stay between the black sky
and the broken hearted

It traveled through my nose and reached the tips of my toes

It spread like wildfire through my lungs

leaving me gasping for air each time

It hit me in the middle of the day

clearing my mind

leaving only thoughts of you and I

memories flooded every corner of my brain

I could feel your hands touching mine and

I don't think your presence had ever felt so real and alive

It stung my eyes and speared my heart

leaving me to bleed out wherever it decided to show

and for months

it never allowed me to let you go

until one day it stopped coming around

I haven't smelled you since

—The ghost of your scent—

I hit you where it hurts so you'd finally learn to feel

I hoped you'd cut me where I healed so I could remember
what it was like to feel

—genie in a bottle, grant my wish—

You only adore me when my clothes are scattered across your floor

and my mouth is closed shut with the pressure of yours against it

with your hand up my shirt

and the other in my pants

You never want me when I spill all of these words
along with a thousand tears that you created

You never want my heart

You just want my body

and how heartbroken I have become in realizing so

It's a line

that goes on forever

And I

remain at the end

This is a different kind of wound

cutting me in places I never knew existed

Replaying images in my head

I only wish I could forget

—*He never gave me the chance to say no*—

It's like every time you're given something that makes you hopeful it's always taken away. At the end of the day the words they say don't mean a thing because they've been used so many times by people who never meant them. You don't know what or who to believe anymore. And that's quite sad because someday someone is going to mean it and maybe by the time that day comes I'll be too cold to accept it. And I pray to God that I never get the chance to witness my heart freezing over.

I spent so much time putting you back together

just for someone to come along and rip each stitch I sewed

apart

in parts of you I had never known existed

I planted flowers where holes once were

he dug them up

the holes bigger than before

New pain has found its home

old pain resurfaced,

so I did what I know best

I grabbed my sewing kit

reached inside my chest

and began stitching you back up

In hopes that this will be the very last time I have to do so

—*Open heart surgery*—

THE
Fallen Star

It was the day you left

you didn't just take your things

and disappear into the night

You packed up everything I loved about myself

and took it with you

leaving me with nothing

While learning you

I lost myself between the blurred lines

By searching for you

I could no longer be found

And when I lost you

I knew I'd never return quite the same

Pieces of my heart are everywhere we've never been

only dreamed about

scattered across the world

in search of the place where our souls meet

but they seem to end up in a different place

each and every time

It started out slowly

but with each passing moment

my body

fell

further

deeper

into the abyss

They're all standing around

but no one seems to notice that I'm drowning

and I'm not too sure how much time I have left

There are times when I find it quite hard to write. Sometimes my happiness is so overwhelming that I simply just can't find the words. And sometimes my sadness is far too much to bear.

—*My pen bleeds nothing*—

Hope runs wildly through my veins

cut me

and I will bleed thousands of stories about heartbreak

and all of the ways it crept into my soul and burned me

Filling my lungs with smoke

Choking me with memories

and visions that I have so desperately tried to rid of

I've searched

high and low

through the smallest of corridors

and the most shattered windows

In every city,

big and small

and every sad

dreary town

but you're nowhere to be found

You can do all things

but you can't seem to keep that smile on your face lately

and you just don't know why

you're too afraid to find out

because the answer might be the thing that finally breaks you

after all this time

They don't look at the small details

or the variation of colors you've chosen

they look past it

painting their own picture of you

And instead of letting the observer observe

they

tear down the artwork you once were and leave you in a pile of lies

and many cases of misunderstanding

because that seems to be where you belong lately

It is terribly lonely within the walls of empty

a place for the unwanted to hide

a sanctuary for the devil to reside

an excuse for me to need you

just one last time

Every time I try to forget you

I remember all of the things we could be

and then I try so hard to remember the sound of your voice

only to lose it all

along with myself

—*A distant memory*—

It's weird to think a year ago we shared this month together. It's weird to think we watched movies and talked about the stars for hours on end. My heart aches to know that I was that close to having you. I miss all of your wonder and soul, all of the songs and little pictures, all of your deep meaningful thoughts that mirrored mine. I miss the face you used to make when you were trying to hold back a laugh so you could crack a joke and the way you always smelled like home. It's even worse to think that was our second chance. I believe everyone enters our lives for a reason, but I hate to believe that your purpose was just to teach me a lesson, because you gave me so much more.

The pain that occurs in my chest when I look at you and realize everything we will never be able to experience together

is unbearable

I'm filled with words but once they hit the page they don't seem to make sense anymore, but you were the only one who understood that.

I drove by your house today

and felt empty

The trees still swayed the same

your car was parked in the driveway

the birds were chirping

your neighbor waved

but one thing did not remain the same,

us

I drove by your house today

I really missed you today

nothing will ever quite be the same

Life without you has lost its spark

I wonder if you feel the same

I drove by your house today

unexpectedly took a trip down memory lane

all the way

praying

things could be okay, someday

I drove by your house today

I can't share these words with anyone,
because no one appreciates them the way you do

I thought you set me free

but you took my expectations

and placed them on the highest shelf

holding my words captive

for only your eyes to see

My dad always told me, "You get what you give."

but he was wrong

because I've given you everything I had

and all you gave me was this hole in my chest
from the heart you so blatantly stole

How can we truly know what is meant to be?

How do I know that letting you go will set me free?

I hate you

not in the punch your shoulder and roll my eyes way

I hate you so much

that my insides ignite into flames

I hate you so much

that I hope your consequences outweigh the damage of your actions

I hate you so much

that when I speak of you

my teeth grit and my eyes go black

I hate you

not in the "I hate you" way

but in the

"I hate you so much that I love you" way

and it doesn't make any sense

—*The logic of my aching, breaking heart.*—

I don't understand why you search the world trying to find something that is right in front of you. Are you honestly that blind? There are people that would sell their soul for you and you're making a fool of yourself by choosing to look at the ground.

Inside there

are incredible things

that I myself can not manage to envision

You

a wonderful masterpiece

Inside your mind I get lost

and oh what a lovely place that is to be

lost and found, within you

your mind has all of my love,

love,

please never let your mind astray at the thought of me

because once you begin to do so

there will be no one left to remember me

Everything that I write, I write for you. But you never come around anymore; so I have all of these poems and excerpts and stories that I want to share with you but you never want to hear them. So the happiness in these stories turns to heartbreak, and you never end up reading the things I've written for you, for us. They just sit on my shelf and collect dust like the few memories you've given me. I've kept them all even though I know you've thrown most of them away, but it's okay, they have a place to stay now.

How can I reach you?

you're so much further than gone

I have climbed the highest mountain

screaming your name,

no answer

not even an echo

I drove the distance

you weren't there

I walked down every street in town

but you were nowhere to be found

Once I did find you, you were all alone

and had not one thing to say

I turned around to walk away

Realizing I had just lost myself along the way

Retracing my steps

I found bits and pieces of her

and spent my long walk home

wondering if I'd ever make it there,

wondering if I'd ever find her again

I can almost hear my heart break

as my tears hit the pillow case

from the pain of many years

I am empty

I am numb

I am everything I hoped I'd never become

I am someone with a shattered soul

I am filled with doubt that the hope I carried for so long
even exists in my world today

I am constantly wishing for all of my yesterdays to somehow change

I am impatiently being patient for all of the wrong people

and things

I am devoid of emotion

because it has been robbed from my possession

I am somehow happy in the midst of all this chaos

It has been how many years

and all I can seem to want to do

is make sure I never forget how badly my need to disappear is

and how badly it wouldn't make a difference if I did or not

it's been the same steady pace of nothing for so long now

I forgot what it was like to be truly missed

The doctors said it was the rarest cause of death
they'd ever come across

in fact

the only encounter in history

They discovered her lying on top of the sheets

unmarked

untouched

still as beautiful as ever

A book filled with her thoughts

pressed tightly to her chest

held by her small blue, now cold fingers

It took them weeks,

months

to figure out the cause of death

Her heart in perfect condition, or so they thought

until they opened up her brain and read her thoughts

Her scripture written over the pages she once held onto so dearly

a single thought on the only marked page of the book

It fell to the floor,

not another word was spoken aloud
until a proper service was held

continued...

where the man with a cross around his neck
spoke words she was never able to speak aloud

"Hope. It is given to those in need of a reason to carry on.
It is provided to the ones who believe so deeply. I was in need
of it for both of these reasons and many more. But the others
involved just wanted to play, and I had nothing left inside
of me. I knew for sure I would not win this game."

Unmarked

Untouched

It never occurred to anyone that

the very reason some are able to live on,
is the cause of another's heart to stop beating

How long is it going to take my heart to accept the fact that you are gone, and never intend on coming back?

It's always right before bed

when thinking of you hurts the most

During the day the presence of other people
is just barely enough to distract me

but your absence can never go unnoticed

Don't worry darling

it's just something we all go through

but she's wrong

this isn't normal

this don't sleep until 5

wake up at 3

not hungry until every soul is asleep

because the thought of their minds being alert

and you not being the mere existence of a thought

kills you

But you can't blame them for not thinking of you
while they're asleep

right?

It keeps you up

but all it ever really does is bring you down

Flowing through your veins like a drug

traveling miles a day from your brain

to your heart

Leaving behind questions with no answers

confusion and loneliness

You spent so much time up there in your head you never
had the chance to make real friends

the ones you have no longer want you

because it's the same thing everyday

ask

answer

repeat

BRENNA KATSOUDAS

It fades so quickly

one minute it's a wide grin

and the next I can barely turn my lips upward

the pain in your stomach when you laugh too hard

aches in my chest

when I pull out the smile that doesn't seem to have a place
on my face anymore

Your biggest fear is dying

but oh how horrifying it is to live

a life lonely

Darling, why are you so afraid to die

when it is a much harder task to stay alive?

I have created a lake

that soon has the potential to become an ocean

and all I can do

is hope that I don't drown in my own sorrows

The words have nowhere to escape to anymore

they just float around in my head

they bounce off of the many sturdy walls I built

how tragic that they never find a way out

We are just simply drifting through life without each other and
how tragic it truly is that we have wasted all of this time apart.

She spent her life falling in love with things she could never have

that's why when he came along

fear took its toll

for all she had to do was snap her fingers

and he would be hers

That terrified her more than dreaming
and hoping of a fairytale for eternity

So she kept him at arm's length

Once she realized how wrong she had been

she started chasing

but he had been long gone

now she only had herself to blame

—*Gone with the wind*—

I read in hopes to escape my mind and rid of all the
memories I hold of you.

I missed this old pen

and tattered paper

I've missed the beautiful words I once so easily strung together

Things this everlasting smile has cost me

So I wished upon plenty of stars for a reason to write

for when I was not very sleepy at night

My wish was his command, so that is what he did

Giving me a reason to create feelings from letters
formed into words, into sentences

By taking away the only thing that was in its place,

happiness

—Opportunity cost—

I am afraid you are so far gone that even now I could never find you

Sometimes I see you in the eyes of the ones I love

but I do not see you in my eyes, where you belong

I didn't see you when he was kind

or when all he wanted was to be close to you

I saw you slipping away in each moment

quicker than the last

I didn't see you on the drive home

when you should have been all smiles

because this is what you've always wanted after all

wasn't it?

What frightens me the most is that I don't see you
when I look in the mirror

In all ways I am kind, and empathetic. If there is anything about myself I am sure of, it is that. I have always sacrificed my own happiness to make sure that everyone else does not suffer the cost. In doing so I have lost myself terribly along the way. I am in far too deep and I keep trying to climb out, but I continue to fall back into who I have become. I feel so drained and absent from everything and everyone. I hate who I am sometimes, but I try to give myself the benefit of the doubt; For I have not always been this way. I will not concede, I must find her again. Thing is, I no longer know where to find her and I fear that she is long gone by now. There are times, like today, where I see her in my actions towards certain individuals that remind of who I was. I see her in certain mood swings I have and I try so hard to make them last, but they never do. I have been calling out. I have been screaming my own name through each corridor. I have been asking strange faces where she has disappeared to but they just stare blankly and continue on their journey. While I am stuck here without her. How can I even manage to go on? I have been trying to save every last piece of her. Talking to God. Please save us.

She,

a fallen star

willing to cross the cosmos

to find her way back home

There once lived a girl

with nothing to her name

not because she was poor

but because she gave it all away

no one said thank you

they didn't even bother to stay

how sad she was when she gave all she had,

body and soul

expecting nothing in return

only to be stripped of her sanity

left in a pile of dust

labeled with her name

The only thing they couldn't manage to take away

If you're trying to hurt me, find another way

it's not going to work

I have been pushed around so many times

I've been kicked to the dirt,

I am numb to the pain

and I know it sounds insane

but I'm so used to this life

It comes in small doses

One sad

lonely night a month

a couple hard days a week

then a few nights crying yourself to sleep

When you talk about the wars raging in your mind

you say: "It's hardly like this anymore."

but what you fail to recognize is

it's seeping back into you

each day

you fight

doing anything to rid of the memory that it was a sad lonely night

Refusing to remember the hard days this week

changing the story so that

crying yourself to sleep was just part of a silly dream

Until your next sad lonely night

when no one is there to hold you

and you think long and hard about losing the fight

I have been staring at myself in mirrors and talking to myself in the dark trying to come to a conclusion as to why I feel so far from myself lately, and I think I found my answer. I have gone through different types of pain all throughout my life, as many people have. From falling off of a bike and scraping my knee to experiencing the death of a loved one. From physical to emotional pain. But I have also realized that the physical pain I have endured has never changed me as a person, whereas the emotional pain has carved me into someone that sometimes I don't even recognize. I can't seem to even express that to anyone but the pen in my hand and the paper I write upon. I have been missing someone for a long time and maybe that person is me.

I've waited all of this time to finally let you go

but now here I am

stuck in a crossfire

between

you

and I

and fate

Time has wedged itself between us

maybe this is what healing feels like

but guilt has taken over

because I'd rather miss you, than let you go

It almost feels as though I've accepted everything

and nothing has ever felt so wrong

Everyone else may not see past the smile

but I do

I see the desperate pain prying apart your jaw to escape
and leaving a frown upon your beautiful face

I see the puddles begin to form in your warm chocolate eyes

I see you try to hide it all

but I hope you know that with me you'll never have to hide

you don't have to hold the pain in,

let it pull away the smile

you don't have to blink away the puddles,

let them splash

Let yourself feel

after all these years

it's the least you could do for yourself

I love you with everything I have inside of me

more than you'll ever know

more than you could ever imagine

but I can't seem to tell you enough anymore

when once upon a time it was all I knew how to do

but every time I form the words in my head

I'm too afraid to let them escape

—Dear Mom and Dad, the world ruined me—

I have caged you up

and locked you away

behind every door

so far from any other beating heart

that you completely forgot what it feels like to love

to feel

And now as you read the words upon the paper
you hold so gently in your hand

you weep

not for the beautiful words of poets who felt more like friends

than strangers,

saving your soul

Instead

you weep for yourself

because even after all of this time

you still haven't fully healed

and you can't help but wonder if you ever will

A ghost

in my own home

striding down the hall

unseen

by the living souls

not only beside, but around

Trapped in a world where no one can see

the one who sees

the world the way it should be seen

I could write a million stories about the broken hearted girl who stares out her window each night looking for something more. I could write you a thousand melodies that will sing you the songs of my aching heart, but nothing will compare to the feeling of being trapped in this small bitter town that is my world. Nothing can amount to the pain I feel when I wake up every morning and go through the same routine, always reminding me of how much I don't belong here. How bad I long to leave, but there is always something that prolongs my stay. I could publish endless amounts of books where the words I have written are drawn up by my tears; But the tenderness of craving to leave will always reside within my soul, because you are never welcome to a place that you do not belong.

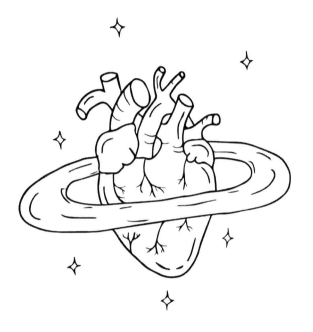

Stardust

I hope not long from today

and not far from tomorrow

you will begin to see

that I was put on earth for you,

as you were for me

I could write about you all day everyday

and the mountains wouldn't dare echo back

One day you are the night sky shining through my soul,

the next

you are the waves in the ocean

knocking me down

teaching me how to pick myself up from your mistakes

The rain, reminding me that everything washes away in time

that I am reborn once the sun shines again

And you held my hand along the way

through our season

but it didn't seem to last long enough

3 syllables

you don't even have a clue

my mind is constantly racing wild with thoughts of you

I can't seem to shake them

I can't think of you without feeling pain strike
straight through my heart like a lightning bolt

And I can't bear to look at you

without tears springing to my eyes

as if it was the very last time I'd ever lay eyes on you

3 little syllables

and I don't think you'll ever know,

because how could I ever tell you?

I didn't ever want to stop breathing you in
because you tasted like oxygen

all things sweet in life

and if I never have the chance again, I hope you know I love you more
than my favorite ice cream on a humid summer day

and I would have handed over all the things I loved,
just so I could keep the thing I loved the most,

you

I would have breathed you in forever

if you hadn't had the nerve to cut off my lifeline

It's easy for you to do cliche things like sing and dance in the rain

It's easy to do anything when you have a good enough reason to

except when the song was ours

and dancing reminds me of how I can't,

I only could when I was with you

and the rain reminds me of the night you left

when not only I cried for us,

but so did the stars

There's just something about the night

that brings the thought of us to life

it burns bright embers in my heart,

scorching them into my mind

As I awake, these memories so vivid,

I fail to recognize the difference between our sweet dreams

and my own dreadful reality

I allowed you to see me in a way

only a few have

Not to be confused

with my body being undressed

You knew my brain

inside

and out

And how terrifying that was for me

and how painful it is now

knowing that you know it all

knowing that you're all gone

Somedays

the only thing my mind knows how to do

is bleed your name

It's 2:16 am. I just got back from my favorite city. I'm absolutely exhausted and I just want to go to sleep, but I can't. My mind has been awoken with thoughts of you. And each one delivers an ache to my heart because you're not here. And oh how I'd love to tell you what it was like. The people. My adventures. But your mind is sound asleep to the thought of me. You are roaming the streets playing silly games with your friends until the clouds of smoke fill your brain and make everything we were a distant, foggy memory.

—*A message from Ms. NYC and I*—

History could repeat itself a million times over

and I'd never complain

If my heart must be broken time

and time again

I'd love for you to continue doing the honors

Is it fate

or merely a coincidence

that we are here again

and it feels as though

nothing has changed

even though we both have, in the best way

Is this in the plan

or will you go away again

and if so

for how long

and why do you never take me with you?

I don't know what it is, but when you're around

the words just spill out of me like a waterfall

and they don't seem to stop

They're always in the right order

and always sound so sweet

and every poem and entry I create

is a thank you note for you to keep

We are connected

not by our parts

but by the love for the music in our hearts

and I hope with everything inside of me

that will be the sole reason we make it through this hurricane
that we have created

with miles

and miles

between us

I spent so many months after you left in a drought of words and poems. After I had poured out all of the sadness it was as if you had taken part of me with you, the most important part of me, my soul. In a writers block for months on end. And just as you returned the drought had ended and it all came back to me. My inspiration. My muse. My love, this is no coincidence.

You're only one person

so how come

you can erase the memory of everyone else,

leaving just the two of us?

Not a night passes by

that I don't imagine myself underneath your touch

begging for more

every inch you shift further away from me

my body cries for you

slowing dying

It never gets a drop

just a couple dreams

I have missed you for eons

my aching was felt in every galaxy across the milky way

in every beating soul

pretending to mask the pain with secret lovers

who were never quite as wonderful as you

—*A thousand light years between us could never keep me from you*—

All of the things I never loved

became flowers around my heart upon meeting you

I had always been a sucker for green eyes

anything other than blue

only for the sole reason that I was convinced they were overrated

But your eyes,

your beautiful blue eyes

pointed lasers at my heart

and burned a hole so deep

that my brain will never be able to forget those eyes,

those beautiful blue eyes

I was never a fan of green leaf magic

but for you

I'd put up with anything

whatever the cost

measure

distance

maybe you could say it was an exception

You

were an exception

my exception

Danger and I did not get along well

but I'd dance with the devil if you'd asked me to

I would have set the world on fire if you said so

continued...

BRENNA KATSOUDAS

and we'd have gotten away with it all

because you were my exception

We had the world at the tips of our fingers

you held it in your palm

and as it spun for us

we lost control

It didn't work with two

only one

because

we are not the exception

It was only ever you

You were the only one possible of lighting up our hearts with that
smile and making the world turn with the sound of your laughter

You could commit every crime in the book

you would always get away with it

murder

they'd never know

You didn't have to think about such a thing

because when you walked out the door that's exactly what you did

As gut wrenching as it is

to have lost my life

I forgave you in an instant

because after all

You are my exception

I write these words

to explain to you what I feel

although I've never had the courage to say them to your face

I hope these don't make it to you too late

You instilled a power in me

I had no recollection of existing

To do all things with the love I had held inside of my heart for eons

saving it all

for the one who could ignite a fire

within my soul

The few words you uttered in the 3am silence brought me to life

Without a second thought

I handed you all of the love I was saving,

with not a care in the world of how bad it was going to hurt in the end

You were deserving of all the love in the world

You opened your eyes to see what everyone else had failed to

giving me everything I had been waiting all these years for

After all you put me through in the end

I still like to think of you the same

My view of you shall never change

I'd like to thank you for bringing the hidden parts of my heart to life

All of this was because of you

It is so incredible to me

that the moment you came back,

so did all of the words I have been struggling trying to find

searching through space,

doing just about anything to kill time

The feeling of longing for something

wanting to go home,

but when home is a person, and you've been locked out

you spend the rest of your life being homesick
for the other half of your soul

Searching the world for a similar feeling

only to end up back on their doorstep

I've always been afraid of addiction

not that I've had any interest in anything
I could become addicted to

but

I haven't ever wanted something so badly
that I couldn't seem to live without it

until I met you

Sometimes I want to write everything I feel about you, but
usually I can't come up with anything other than I love you.

Humans need other humans

it's not a weakness

it's not degrading

it's not that you can't be on your own

it's that we weren't meant to be alone

There would be no us if it was just Adam

or just Eve

Humans need humans

and there is nothing wrong with that

Sometimes you need another heart to make yours
beat just a little longer

I have never missed a season more than a few autumns ago

every waking second spent in your presence

keeping the gaping hole in my heart company

mending me back together as each leaf fell
from the lonesome tree in your window

I never had to ask, you always knew exactly what to do

After all that's what best friends are for

I'm not sure why I always think of you

there must be a reason

because there are billions of people in this world

and I've laid eyes on a million faces

but yours is the one I always come back to

Admired for your beauty,

as you should be

Overlooked for your insides

which hold the key to all unanswered questions

The color of the earth glistens in your eyes

and reveals a passion for a man who is not deserving of the answers

but you and I both know he needs them

so you allow him full access as he fills your heart
with both joy and sadness

but with every drop of sadness you begin to wonder if it will ever be
worth the smile he ever so rarely grants access to crack upon his face

letting his broken pieces fit into yours

made for each other,

or so it once seemed

The answers you have, had always been the love he needed,
but took for granted

adding to the strength you've always had

allowing you to let someone go who will never amount
to the love your heart deserves

We shouldn't have to fight, it should just be. You should want me because you need me, not because you feel like you should need me. And I should want you because you're right for me, not because I want you to be right for me.

A world of endless possibilities,

I waste

remaining here

awaiting the possibility

that you could love me

in this town

I've always wanted to escape,

but would stay

for you

I believed in you

in every single word you spoke

all of the things we said we'd do

I believed that you would love someone extraordinary in this world,
whether or not that was me

Most of all I believed in your heart

until

your words changed over time to fit who you had become

Instead of loving someone worth your while, you loved someone
who valued the body more than the heart

Instead of being you,

you became him

And I'm not so sure who he is

Sometimes I want to write so viciously and wild
that my pen breaks along with your heart,

while mine heals and learns to love someone
a millions times better than you.

My heart aches for the version of you I dreamt up
in my head while the world was asleep

My heart aches for both versions of myself,

because neither of us can let you go

It is ultimately impossible to forget someone who
has made you feel as though you were worthy of the
world and all of it's wonderfully hidden possessions.

I have told just about every paper that this pen
has landed on how much I long for you

I have prayed that one of these pages, or poems,
would have made it to you by now

but as I see they haven't

I will continue to brag about your beauty
to every blank lonely page my pen comes across

I've become remarkably great at acting like I don't miss you,
like I don't still dream about you

I have spent months denying it

I have searched for someone just like you so I wouldn't cry anymore,

so I'd stop missing you

I have spent months convincing myself

I don't

when I know damn well I do

I have felt wonders

and dreamt them up with you

I have come alive

at the thought of your touch

I have lived through your image

I have felt your heartbeat

your hands on my skin

setting me ablaze

creating life

making a story

Dreaming us into reality is the closest I have come to kissing your lips

and trembling beneath your touch

I dream through you every night

Because it's the only way I know how to fall asleep

All of my favorite places

turned into ours upon meeting you

All of this time apart

so close in distance

so far away in time

All of the places I found peace in

became graveyards for all of the memories we would never make

and all of those graveyards became a home to my lonely heart

because after all of this time

I've never felt you more than I have in these passing moments

and I've spent my entire life chasing ghosts

and I would chase yours forever if it's the only piece of you I'll ever get

If I wrote to forget you

I wouldn't be driving past your house every time I missed you

I shouldn't complain, I had the luxury of waking up this morning

and although it wasn't by your side

I've had the pleasure of knowing you

I'd hate to settle for just that

but it seems that's all I'll get in this lifetime

As little of an impact it is that I have on you

You open windows and shut doors

you allow me to breathe in the fresh air of your lungs

and it saves my soul from the thoughts surrounding my head

My eyes flutter awake with you on my mind

although we haven't spoken two words in the last 8 months

I try to breath a new name

but they don't sound quite the same as you do

Attempting to find new faces in each crowd

only to find your smile sitting upon every stranger

Maybe I will never escape your presence

for I seem to be cursed by your ghost

As much as I'd like to be angry about such a thing

I can't help but smile knowing you'll always be within me

How tragic of me to talk as if you've passed

hoping I will never see the day you do

And just a reminder before you fall asleep tonight,

I can guarantee that I will always love you

You call them poems

I call them love letters in disguise

addressed to all, only meant for

you

The thought of you

sparks a thousand images, a million words

everything you do makes me want to write

everything you are makes me want to be better

—You are my inspiration—

You never failed to make me feel as though every word I wrote could
end the wars going on in the minds of the broken hearted

Anything less than that has never been worth my time,

which is why I chose to keep my words hidden in pages like these

I'm sorry for bothering you

I don't mean to be such a burden

You're just my favorite person to bother

and if I could be of anything to you

I'll take being a burden

over being absolutely

nothing

To say the absolute least, I've missed you oh so dearly

There is not one single day that has gone by
where I have not loved you

—Well I could love you forever and that still wouldn't be enough—

Don't think I didn't notice babe

when the smile slowly fades away from your loving face

And you can take mine along with it

because

your happiness is mine

we share this heart for the rest of our lives,

If you can't be happy, why should I?

—Says Romeo to Juliet—

My favorite part is when

you're laughing

and I'm laughing

and I look away

but you just keep staring at me with those deep blue eyes of yours

immediately melting my heart into a defenseless puddle

filling me with this happiness that I can't seem to describe,

and I think maybe someday we can love each other

Everything about him makes me write

It all begins and ends with him

Although I have the power

although I have the talent

he just looks at me and poems rain from the sky

He is poetry

I am poetry

We are poetry

In the night

do you dream of me in the sweetest of dreams?

And while awake do you count down the hours
until you can dream of me again?

I have never looked into eyes that begged me not
to look away, until I looked into yours.

Unless I've been mistaken

I think I saw a gleam of affection within your eyes,

but I'm almost always incorrect

for it was probably just the

reflection of mine

The stars were shining so bright that night

I remember because I saw them in your eyes

When the air turns crisp

and the leaves begin to fall

I am reminded of each time your mind occupied mine

Once upon an October moon

and a few September stars

I'm scared that I will have to go through life knowing
you are the one and never being able to have you

I could spend the rest of my life writing love letters to you,

but I'd rather just tell you

I dreamt of a love so wild and pure

each night before slumber

slipping into a world of my own

inviting sleep to take over my lonely body

pulling me into someone

with a blank

nameless face

Countless nights spent dreaming the same dream

except,

when the opportunity was placed in my hands

I struggled to keep hold of such a thing

letting it slip away

completely unaware how difficult it is

to hold two hearts on one leash

when they're both going in different directions

at different paces

with the same intention

I am writing this to you 11 years later

not quite sure what to say

with absolutely no intention of your eyes ever landing on these pages

I am writing this to you, finally,

after each failed attempt I hid under my bed in hopes
that if I'd forgot you existed, so would my heart

I am writing this to you because

11 years ago

I fell in love with those chocolate eyes

that matched that chocolate hair of yours

Causing magic to course through my bloodstream

Leaving me in a permanent daze for the next

11 years

so young

yet so hopelessly infatuated with the fairytale of us

11 years

full of almost's and what could have been's

11 years ago

and I never saw today coming

The day when two distant worlds would pass through the same time zone

filled with

11 years of built up desire

I am writing this to you because for the past 11 years you have made
your way in and out of my heart and brain like a revolving door

For the past 11 years, I let you

Pieces of the past

why do you run

when all the signs point to us?

There doesn't seem to be a place for me anymore in your heart

not that there ever was

but in my mind you had a place for me

while down here on earth I always had one for you

Just as easy as you fall in it,

you can fall back out

Just as easy as you felt everything,

you can feel nothing at all

SUPERNOVAS OF THE HEART

After being ignored

mistreated

and

lost within your corridors

I still chose you

on my darkest days

in my loneliest nights

right or wrong

love or hate

it was always you

I think I will always love the people

that do not love me

because everyone needs love

even the ones not capable of showing it

You may not have the power to love me,

or anyone else for that matter

but I was built with enough love to withstand each storm
inside of your tired, aching bones

and this time I've even saved enough for myself

so we can survive this round together

—*Love has wings*—

I believe in everyone

and everything

I bleed faith

I breathe hope

And as wonderful of a thing it is

oxygen sometimes fails to reach my heart

I have come to accept that I will always carry the burden
of every heart I've ever know

and every heart ever known

for I am the blood in each and every vein

I am the power within the caged animal that lies in your chest

I've given you all the gift of love

so now I must suffer the consequences

Here, I present to you,

my heart

My love for you is like rain in the desert

rare to come across, valuable as gold

My love for you is taken for granted

Pouring all of me into something,

someone,

who can't absorb it

While you claim it never rains here in this desert

And I will spend my life searching the world for the love
you gave me, in someone else,

since you seem to have lost it

I am in love with space and the way everything
in this world is based on fate

How I was meant to love you

and you were meant to love her

and the tragedy of it all

I dream of you often. Sometimes you have a different face, but always the same warm familiar heart. I wonder if this is how the rest of my life will go, only ever dreaming of you. Will it be enough to keep me going? Looking back on the September days we spent together. How a year ago on this very day we talked and laughed about everything under the sun. And I missed you already because somewhere deep down, I always knew we were destined to end.

You asked if my heart had ever been broken

I answered with a yes

and told you that it had been my own fault

that I had broken my own heart

You said you understood

that it did indeed make sense

And then you took it upon yourself to change my answer

now the only person I have left to blame

is myself

I wish that one person did not have the ability to ruin so many things for you. And I wish that one name did not have the power to make your heart break all over again. And I wish more than anything that I could take it all away. But I can't erase your memories or the mess he chose to make. And I can't reach into his heart and take back the piece of yours that he stole, just so I could give it back to you. But you have to know, if I could, I would.

—To my best friends heart that I spent forever trying to mend.—

I'm not sure how

or why

but you always know

when my heart is aching

when it's broken and needs taping

And for this I will be eternally grateful

that God connected our hearts

and made sure you were always there to save mine from falling apart

This way it begins to fall

but the only sound it makes

is the beating that it continues to do

and darling, that is all because of you

Sharing becomes a whole new concept when it no longer refers to inanimate objects. Sharing a person and their time is difficult in ways you cannot understand, until your very best friend becomes his whole world. And you have to learn to let it go.

—*I'm thankful it hurts this much, I'm thankful I have you.*—

I am fearless, yet I am terrified of you

Your presence is alarming,

powerful

All you'd have to do was look my way and I'd fall at your feet

I am fearless

yet I am terrified of falling in love with you

How fascinating

brought here, together by God

as he watches our story from above

Like a book he has already read

or a movie he has already watched

Finally making it to the big screen

for the rest of this marvelous world to see

This is the tale of Bonnie and Clyde
two fierce lovers who put their morals aside,
gathered up the money,
took a few lives,
broke each other's hearts
and left this world behind
painting death and tainted love in the brightest colors across the sky

That's what we spend our days searching for,
the kind of love that engulfs you
It's only infatuation when you're in love with the idea, the thought,
but darling I'm in love with you

My imagination isn't enough anymore
I want you to touch me everywhere
In all of the places that have been longing for you
every inch of my skin
and every corner of my heart

How many more meaningless interactions do you and I need to have until one of us realizes this is silly? That all of those coincidences weren't just little accidents created by the universe. You and I; intentionally placed here at this time and place by none other than fate herself. Unaware that we had more power in our two souls combined than Romeo and Juliet had in a lifetime. We created stories with our eyes and drew up fantasies with our lips. Except we never had to dream of better days, we were the better days. We dreamt with our eyes wide open and our hearts on fire.

Doomed from the start

your eyes laying me down, finding every secret
I hid from you all of these years

my heart freeing the chains from yours

As I discovered all of the flowers in your garden

truly amazed at the sight

You picked a few

and laid them down beside me that night

Baffled at the consequences, as your hands bled from the thorns

You handed me your garden

and I finally agreed to put down my sword

As if I were a window, without a shade

Your ocean eyes gazed ever so deeply into my soul

Seeking out the parts of me I could never find

bringing them to life

There's something about him that makes the poetry spill from my lips

and roll off my tongue

as if I was meant to speak his language

—He is poetry—

I fought for you my entire life, so believe me when I say now that I have you I will never let you go.

—Dear future lover—

"Touch me." she said.

"Make up for all of the years I spent dreaming up nights like this where you and I would finally collide."

Covered by the light of a midnight sky

dancing among the fireflies

and moonlight in your eyes

I once dreamt of what we could be

hidden beneath the trees

where no one could see your arms wrapped oh so tightly around me

In a place where the planets revolved around our hearts

we would move the world with love

And they'd all stop and stare at the moonlit stardust drops in your hair

as comets soared across our sky lighting the hearts of the world on fire

our kisses creating supernovas blinding to the human eye

But we kept our eyes closed

because the best things in life are felt with our eyelids
pressed tightly together

Our love was felt in every galaxy

in every beating heart

And all we had to do was dance

Celestial

Happiness is quite contagious around you my love

it enters my veins

infiltrates my body

fills my lungs

The tune of your voice rings eternally throughout my ears

It runs so deep, my blood turns yellow

Tell me again

how the light hits my face in a dark room

How even in the blackest of nights

my smile still lights up the world

The damned and the beautiful

except she is both

One moment the tears threatening to spill

creating a tsunami

and then

laughter as pure as a newborn

creating double rainbows across the sky,

and that's why I'll never understand

why humans question the change in weather

—*Sunshine mixed with a little hurricane*—

I can't sleep

because

I am overwhelmed with happiness

over the simple thought that

when you're not asleep

I am the one you choose to talk to

about all of the beautiful things in life,

like

how my eyes shine when you speak wondrous words

and

how your heart races when you make the
mile wide smile appear upon my face

Or how you're the moon

and I'm the stars

And you know just how much I love the moon

Do you remember our days spent in the field

loving each other among the daisies

as comets soared across our midnight sky

As I walk this field alone tonight, the crickets chirp

reminding me of all the times we felt alive

Maybe these lines hide secret messages
that I have spent hours stringing together,

just so the day you came across them your heart would
weep my name, as I have for you. These are meant for
you, but I'm sure you already knew that.

You make me feel everything all at once,

that is why it's so hard to keep this pen out of my hand

BRENNA KATSOUDAS

God created the stars and he created humans as well, but with you he put a little bit of both, and that's why you shine so much brighter than the rest of us.

Droplets fall slowly

hitting the delicate paper

with a splash

Words become blurred

time becomes frozen

emotions overflowing

beautiful words

strung together

to make the heart skip a beat

falter to a stop

and be reborn again

A tragic masterpiece

The magic that lives inside

The beauty of a book

I hope as you continue to read on I make you feel something, because if you are reading and feeling nothing then you might as well stop; these words are nothing more than squiggly lines on tattered paper.

Beautiful girl

you speak such sweet words,

every time you talk

poetry falls from your lips

I walk your path

through the trees

around the river

I smile at your strangers

finding peace within the company they bring as they stroll past me,

destined for their own passage through your weeping willow trees

You are serenity

the place I go when I feel I do not belong

your critters befriend me, surrounding me with life

stirring up the leaves

reminding me that, I too, am one with this path

A portal to a world of wonder

where the oxygen runs wild with fire, inviting all walks of life to tread
its trail into the uncharted territory of mother nature's heart

How a small being that walks this gravel road would be
greatly missed at the slightest chance that she could vanish

And the birds would no longer sing their song

for she is the reason this path continues to go on

and on

and on

—*The place my bench occupies*—

Have you ever witnessed 9:00 am on a September Saturday?

Crisp leaves blowing in the wind

the smell of apple pie in the air

Have you ever witnessed 4:00 pm on a January Tuesday?

Snowflakes falling

peaceful and still

Have you ever witnessed 6:00 am on a May Morning?

Birds chirping, all animals alive

while the warm spring sun hangs high in the sky

Have you ever witnessed 7:00 pm on a July Friday night?

Laughter louder than the music on the radio

love sweeter than the taste of vanilla ice cream stained lips

Have you ever witnessed life in the midst of a magnificent moment?

Have you ever stopped to take it all in?

The beauty that is this world

How incredible that God created it all for our eyes to see,

for our souls to cherish

Happiness lives within my soul

There are moments where the amount of love given off by the people around me is so intense, that I almost feel my heart break for the times when that precious force is not embraced with every fiber of our being.

It's the failed attempt to sleep because
you're too excited for the next day

It's because you're finally going on vacation
and you've been dying this whole time just to get away

The lack of sleep puddled under your eyes in dark purple, heavy lines

quickly replaced by a seed of happiness

because it is always worth losing sleep,

especially when it has everything to do with you

Imagine us in a field of poppies

dancing with the flowers

teaching them how to love

There is nothing as satisfying as looking down at the way your white shoes reflect off of your sun kissed skin. The way your sundress falls over your body so softly, so loosely, letting the summer air touch as much skin as it possibly desires. The feeling of your long hair draped over your shoulders as the sun beats down on you from outside the car window. The breeze blowing back your hair as the sun begins creating a new freckle everyday. The power of wearing sunglasses that makes you believe you could stare at him for eternity and he'd never notice, but he does. Getting goosebumps, not from the night air, but from his presence. Smiling so hard your cheeks turn red adding to the sunburn just below your eyes. Giving him a thousand and one reasons to fall in love with you a million times more than he did last summer time.

If I end up with nothing, I'll always have my words. And I can create new worlds upon my sentences; And I will breathe life into each and every thing so we all have a chance at life again.

—A girl and her best friend, pen and paper—

Sometimes I write such beautiful poems; I can't even fathom how my heart spoke such words and my mind just knew how to sew them together to make tragedy sound so pretty and irresistible.

I have so much to say

but the words never seem to come out of my mouth

so I write them down

right here

so that you can read them

in hopes that maybe someday

they'll mean something to you

You spoke words of wisdom on a blustery afternoon

and my heart began to melt along
with the snow outside of our window

It has been eons since I had heard such
sweet poetry spoken from lips other than my own

Melting icebergs and making flowers bloom was your specialty

—You make me feel celestial—

He saw everything I thought I was so good at hiding and shown a spotlight on it. Calling me out in the open and allowing the rawness of my wounds to be felt. He saw me. Truly saw me. And how freeing and absolutely terrifying it was to have been pried open in broad daylight, in front of my very own eyes. Undressing myself down to nothing would have been quite easier than feeling each stitch he poked at. He gave me what I have always wanted, to be seen. He just knew. He just looks at me and he knows. I could go on about him forever and it wouldn't be long enough. He has the mightiest ability to read my inside thoughts and feelings. And when our eyes meet I am wholeheartedly captivated as the waves crash over the shore in his eyes. When I look through his I see the me he sees, and God I have never looked so beautiful.

Do me a favor

close your eyes

and tell me the first thing you see

when you think of me

Is it yellow?

THE
Wisdom
OF
THE *Moon*

The sun doesn't even try to be spectacular

she just wakes up

and brings all of the light she has to offer the world

and the moon already loves her

Written in the stars

you and I

A story painted vividly in pastel colors across the sky

Held ever so carefully by the moon

brighter than any constellation,

the magnificent tragedy of you and I

I look up to the sky

and realize I am closer to the stars than I will ever be to you

Eons away in other galaxies

they find ways to warm my heart

When will we realize

that our hearts are halves

drifting through space

in search of one another

It's nights like these where I try to make myself believe that

the stars are shining for me

It may just be a fantasy

or it may be the only thing keeping me alright

tonight

because

ever since you left

I've been searching for you everywhere I go

in melodies

and constellations

and in many worlds

far

far

away

Every moment that the sun rises you begin to drift further away

when the sun sets you're almost gone

by the time mid morning comes

you're so far out of sight no one would even know you had been here

except for me,

I'll always remember you

BRENNA KATSOUDAS

And none of this makes sense

nothing makes sense anymore

because I love the stars and the moon

and you said you did too

but now I can't even look at the stars

or cry to the moon

because all I ever see is you

everywhere I go,

in everything I do

You never sleep

because you can't stop wondering,

wondering why it's always you

always the one left behind

no one seems to notice

only you

and the quiet whispers between the stars and the moon

Maybe you'll never know what it's like to bleed out
for the empty hearts of the world

It's just something I've learned from the moon
and his many twinkling stars

Don't tear yourself apart

trying to love someone

who doesn't love anything enough

to give your heart

everything

it deserves

—*Love letters from the moon*—

A breath of fresh air is what it was

to have been miles from the place I grew

Not a familiar face in sight

not a trace of you to be found in this new found town

except even way out here

the birds still sing your name

and the midnight stars still spell out your name in the sky

The universe never failing to remind me that no matter how far I go

or how hard I try to hide

you will always be there

*—I could travel through the Milky Way, Andromeda and back,
and you'd still be within every star.—*

If the moon is too cold for hands to touch

and the sun destroys all that it touches

than I am the sun

and you are the moon

While my soul burns too bright for anyone to handle

yours keeps light hidden

and turns cold to all that show you love

because

it's always dark on your side

you're too afraid to let light come in and change your heart

because it used to be warm,

but that was once upon another moon

You will never know me

You can read my words,

cry a thousand tears,

then see my face

and wonder how such a woman of pure sunshine
could feel such pain

But that is what they don't tell you

Rain may come from the clouds

but it is the sun that feels the misery of the storm

and it is the moon that silences her cries

so that she can rise again and be a beacon for the children
who feel eternal sorrow in the daylight

Do you feel the weight of a thousand galaxies on your shoulder?

Struggling to keep them all alive

Do you carry the weight of the worlds broken hearts
within the cracks in yours?

Searching for the glue that holds the universe together,

only to realize it's been you all along?

I sit quietly at night

spilling my heart to the crescent shaped light in the sky

as he draws out all of the answers to my aching heart

in constellations across the sky

I look up and see the whole world staring back at me,

giving me the strength to go on

Do you ever think about the moon and how it never sleeps?

Even while the sun is burning bright, the moon is still visible

and that is so incredible

Everyone raves about the sun, but the sun rests while the moon shines

It's almost as if he is always watching out for the world

And when you see him hanging up in the sky
he always seems to be smiling

he never has anything to complain about, the stars keep him happy

Not many seem to notice this, which is quite sad

because

Sometimes the sun takes a break while it rains

but the moon never takes a break

and oh how selfless he is for allowing the sun
to take all of the credit for the beauty in the sky

The moon teaches us that sometimes you have to hide out for
a little while in order to let someone else shine for the world.

They say I write about the moon to often

but I disagree

There can never be too much moonlight

You can never get tired of your home

Up there in the sky

is where I found my peace

among the stars

on top of the moon

The one thing that had never let me down

always remaining in the sky,

each and every night

he came out

and made me feel alive

Hand me that pen

let my words dance across these pages

as the stars do across a midnight sky

Between the hours of 12 and 3

the poet picks up her pen

and writes melodies

among the stars in the sky

reminding them of their purpose

the reason they come alive each night

the only form of life

to know that she and her poems exist

The moon spoke to me in phases,

spilling the secrets of the stars that led me to you

I found eternity in your smile and promises in your eyes

unspoken words for the lovers of the land

a gift from above

an infinite amount of moments

in one single passing time

we held each other's gaze

as the stars danced across the sky

to the harmony our love created

singing lullabies to the moon

spreading through galaxies for years to come

pixie dust coating the lives of the ones we love

showering the world with a feeling

a million light years a minute to the heart

and straight back to the core of us

We made love in the cosmos

and the stars thanked us

by sprinkling their dust to the souls below

making them dance among the midnight sky

as our figure displayed in thousands of constellations across the sky

The moon wrapped his arms around me tightly and whispered in my ear "Look up, they're all shining for you."

THE
Unknown

She was the colors in the clouds

the prettiest sunset on her happiest days

warm

God's most precious creation

but she could create a storm so strong

the wind would knock houses down

and rip apart towns for miles

He was the frigid air on a December evening,

the fiercest wind on his most intense days

And he would stir up the leaves beneath her feet

creating friction within their world

setting the world up for disaster

all in the name of their twisted, toxic love

She was fire

He was ice

Pain fueled passion

a sin upon the paper I write

the only time I am capable of creating such beauty

—*half past midnight*—

"I do it all for you" she said.

The lovely words,

the breathtaking images

Openly handing you the key

as you walk by

not even bothering to lift your head and enjoy the view

how my eyes light up at the sight of yours

I thought I could make you sound kinder if I drew you up in pretty words and ribbons and bow ties. I thought time would change you and teach you how to love me.

—But some miracles take an awfully long time—

I can deal with the change in seasons

from warm to cold

I can deal with the transition

of day to night

light to dark

but I cannot adjust to the constant absence of you

Here when you're here

Gone when you're gone

The ease in your step

the day you left

all those years ago

made a reappearance

the day you returned

only a few short moments ago

A swift walk with your head held high

a pair of lonely, cold, empty eyes

looking for a vacancy in mine

All too familiar

and curious at once

I welcomed your stay, even hung your coat up

My expectations at low

as the gates I built around my heart began to open up

allowing your presence to infiltrate my lungs and poison my veins

The thought of you touching me set my heart arace

You

something I only dared to dream of with the lights off

and my eyes closed

I never expected you to invade my reality

Two worlds colliding

continued...

only to be torn apart once again

For I saw this coming in your swift walk towards me

because at the sight of you it was clear that nothing had changed

Our law of attraction was simply based on falling back into old habits.

I,

no more than a vacation spot to you

A trip,

something to clear your head

A sense of home,

for this is ours, except we do not represent each others

A memory

bringing you back to the old times

when you had it all

and I had nothing

The ease in your step

the day you left

all those many years ago

made a reappearance

the day you fled

only a few short memories ago

It's like missing the train as it pulls out of the station

Or when the bus passes your house as you're running towards it

The light turning red as you were so close to making it through

It's the small millisecond where time

overlaps with fate

The slight chance that you've missed something
because it wasn't meant for you

Except you and I fill the grey area between right and wrong

neither one of us knows where to stand

so we fill the unknown with our presence

inches away from one another

but light years

and light years

apart

History has captured my memories holding them captive

until the sun rises in the morn from the abyss

reminding me of all the reasons I should have forgotten you

We shall meet again

When the sun is a little brighter

and your heart has grown warmer

and you have grown endless fields of flowers from the love you finally
feel for me

Oh how tragic

it would be

if my garden had dried up under the infinite amounts of sun I gave it
all those years

I never meant to leave them in a drought

I guess I ran out of tears after quite some time

Dear God,

why did it take him so long?

—It's never too late, or is it?—

I feel many things

but I don't just feel them,

I become them

I live through these feelings

they mold me into someone who not only will understand you

but will feel your pain with you, for you

while managing to keep us both standing strong
on this treacherous ground we call home

18 and graduating does not mean you have grown up

Buying your first car

Getting your first job

does not mean you're growing up

Growing up is having your world turned upside down
when you lose the only thing you never imagined you could,

Yourself

You speak

but the words that fall from your lips

never reach the ears of another soul

And the storm in your brain

never reaches calm

because they don't bother to settle it down

The words you wish to speak

trapped in a memory

locked in a box

Useless and lonely

your heart becomes occupied by darkness

thoughts of no longer existing often cross the streets of your mind

And no one worries about you

because the smile plastered on your sweet face is a mask
for the eternal ache your heart feels

when not a single soul could care any less
about the unsteady beat of the wild beast inside your chest

They don't seem to care enough until it's time to lay you to rest

It is not you,

for it is ghost of regret that haunts their halls

It was the summer of milkshakes that cured
the sadness living in our souls

Occupying each other's empty hearts on our loneliest nights

Lying in the world's comfiest bed wondering
when the aching would end

Side by side spilling the rivers those two boys had created in our eyes

Sipping through a small plastic straw

tasting the sweetness of cotton candy and mint chip ice cream

wishing that one day soon enough

we would find someone just as lovely

but for now

midnight trips to anywhere but that town would have to do

We were never really alone though,

you and I always had each other

—B&B—

She struggles herself, with the words that can make everything okay

but she manages to mend my heart

as her own breaks

so we each pick up a piece and help each other
put ourselves back together

—One piece at a time—

Digging up poetry

from the ruins you left my heart in

I do not hate the girl in the mirror

in fact, I love her,

I always have

It just took me some time to fall IN love with her

The way her eyes shine when she's in love with life,

that was the easy part

There are so many things that I fell in love with so easily

The way her laugh sounded when she finally
set it free was a bit more difficult,

but now I can't imagine my life without it

All of her little things

the very reason that when I look into the mirror

I fall in love all over again

I am more than my body

I am more than my face

I am 100% my heart and brain

My skin is just a pretty mask to cover the unknown that is my soul

Get to know the me you cannot see through the screen of your phone

Meet me in my favorite bookstore beneath the stars,
then maybe we'll talk,

otherwise leave me the hell alone

Everyday I can't help but wonder where you are and what you're thinking, who you're with and what you're doing. But most of all I wonder if you're out there looking for me as much as I'm looking for you.

You have silenced me, in fear that someone may hear me

There are so many wonderful

exotic things

to be excited about in this world

but they are often always overlooked

by the gruesome

painstaking reality

that evil exists

How can such hate

exist in a world

where love and hope

are the only two things that seem to be keeping us all together

I wish to disappear away to a world

where promises mean everything

and lies mean nothing

Keep your eyes closed and mouth shut, they said

feeding hateful words into my head

You shall walk in this line

talk this way

wear these clothes,

and if you ever fall astray

just remember

your own thoughts will never count

for they are incorrect

there is no place for them now

pack them up

I'll take the key

You must breathe my words,

think like me

If you fail these tasks at once

you will live in fear of the rest of us

There is no room in this big old world

for people like you to express your thoughts

continued...

I have burned the key

it is melted now

It I were you I'd keep my voice down

Just a mound of useless opinions

with no one to listen

Day in and out fed with lies

I chose to live my life in spite of it all

to go down with pride and a mind of my own

Live free or die trying

the only way I'll ever choose to go

—*They will try to brainwash you, never allow them the power*—

I talked about people like you to my father

telling him I'd never associate with boys of your kind

the ones who live to smoke

and smoke to live

the ones who do a line for every breath they've ever taken

and breathe in white lines more than they breathe in oxygen

telling him I'd never be apart of someone's heart

who chose drugs over love

and oh what a hypocrite I once was

By walking away

You taught me how to live without you

There is no one to blame but yourself,

I hate that you made me do this

I tell them you disappeared yet again

but you didn't disappear

I know exactly where you are

I'd do anything to try and reach you,

but I know you wouldn't want me to find you

There is something so tragic about the honesty in truth

It's like when you walk in to the library

just browsing

In need of something new, you just don't know what

so you pick up a book and read the back

it intrigues you

You borrow the book

It opens up it's story to you

page

by page,

but before you make it to chapter 3
you realize it's not what you want

so you close the book

and lose interest

you return the book without a second thought

continued...

...continued

I am that book

Everyone who has ever wanted to know me opens my heart,
but never makes it further than 3 steps

They expect something exquisite, wonderfully peculiar.

That's all I've ever wanted to be

But if all of those things were true
I wouldn't be stuck here on this shelf

forgotten

waiting for someone to come pick me up

So I sit here and collect dust

hoping that someday, someone will come along and choose me

and make me feel as though I am
the best book to have ever been written

This lonely bench

cold and empty

where few have taken this place beside me

speaking words I've wanted to hear

but they don't see me, and they don't stay long

Although they didn't keep me much company

loneliness invites itself to occupy the empty seat beside me

some goodbyes affect me more than others

yours has created the biggest void

Making yourself comfortable beside me on this bench

I saw your soul instantly

as you began to see mine, which is something I was not used to

You stayed a while, almost long enough to make me believe you'd
never actually go

but the more you saw, the further you became

Frozen mid decision

as I silently begged you to never leave

continued...

BRENNA KATSOUDAS

I can't see the sun

people continue to pass by

they can't see me

I think you're already gone

You're heart too pure, your mind too cowardly

failing to have let me know that what has begun, has now ended

This bench will never be the same

so I rest my feet in the space you once occupied

now vacated

I miss you most of all

I hope one day you'll return

I've watched you grow from the ground up

I've watched you change from the inside out

I've witnessed you sacrifice the greatest parts of yourself to please others

I've watched you accomplish your greatest goal

I've watched you fall and struggle to pick yourself up

I've cheered you on all along the way, but you never heard me

because I watched your life play out from backstage

Not a single soul on this earth has cared about me
nearly as much as I have cared about them.

—The recurring thought that haunts me—

If this is the last thing I write

I just want you to know

I've missed you with all of my

today's

yesterdays

and tomorrows

And if there's any last words I could say to ease the ache in your heart

It is that

this world has always been enough for me

although I hadn't been much of anything for it

You were my entire universe

I'll carry us through eternity

If there's one last thing you can do

Please never forget me

Why do you try your hardest to convince yourself that they don't love you? Why do you overthink until there is absolutely nothing left of you? Why when you are happy do you force yourself to feel pain? You do not deserve to make yourself feel this way.

I have to go for a while. It's nothing you've done alone, it's something everyone has done. The seasons come and go, and my happiness may be at stake as well. Old habits are resurfacing. Pain is gaining hold of me again. I'm losing grip of the things I know in my heart. It's too hard to stay sometimes. Sometimes I want to leave, but not actually go. No one can stop the hurt, only you. But you're not here sometimes and I know it's not on purpose. But I need you. I'm falling again and right now I don't want to save myself. It all feels familiar but at the same time I'm numb. I hear the thoughts but I don't have the courage to feel them anymore, and this is why I must go. Please forgive me, I'll be back someday soon. I'm sure you won't miss me much because when I'm here it doesn't seem enough. Don't frown or shed a single tear, we all knew this was coming. I hope to see you soon and I hope the rest of your days without me are full of love and happiness. I love you most in this world and I've tried to convince myself that I don't need to do this but there seems to be no other way. I love you I love you I love you, please never forget.

—Not a suicide note—

You asked me why I write,

I simply told you it was because

the mess of thoughts didn't make sense in my head

unless they were strung across empty pages

in beautiful swirly letters

to help mend the shattered souls of our world

—*I make tragedy sound breathtaking*—

Sit on the floor of the shower with your back to the scalding hot water,

free your mind,

and allow yourself to become clean of all the fear tainting your skin

I've gotten quite selfish with the books I come across. You see, I find something that I so deeply relate to, something that I find so beautiful and I decide that I don't want anyone else to know about it. How selfish is that? To hide a marvelous book away from the world all because I want it to myself. But then again, I write all of these extraordinary words that I have never shared with a single soul, until now.

It comes as quickly as it goes,

so I carry you with me everywhere I go

—*The world traveling journal*—

As we grew

I watched my favorite parts of you fade

You packed them all up and tucked them away

as if you never happened

You dimmed all of your lights

and shut all of the blinds

forcing everyone to forget you

replacing the smile on your face with an eternal frown

Your tough exterior became solid stone

Years had passed

you still remained

standing cold and strong

above the darkness you created

in the same place you buried your heart

Now lost and lonely

you found your way to me

unaware

that all of this time

I saved one of my lights

for you

The stone began to crack

your smile reappeared

it would only be a matter of time before you
became everything you had been hiding all of those years

SUPERNOVAS OF THE HEART

When you fall in love with someone you see them everywhere and in everything. Have you ever heard a song and thought of yourself? Have you ever come across something in a small shop that warmed your heart because the first person it made you think of was yourself? Have you ever been so happy to wake up in the morning just to spend the whole day in your own company? Have you ever looked in the mirror and fallen in love with the sweet girl staring back?

I am Gatsby

throwing elaborate parties with this poetry of mine

anything to get you to notice

that we still exist in the same world,

as we always will

How long is it going to take for you to recognize
this green light I've kept alive for us all these years?

I can form words in the prettiest of curly letters

I can pour my heart out to a blank sheet of paper using ink I derived
from my dried up tears and mascara stains,

but there is nothing in this world I can do to make you feel them

You will never be the one to read the beautiful words I am forced to
scribble across tear stained pages at 4 am until my fingers bleed

You will never be there to wipe those tears away as I read my
heartbreak over and over until I am nothing but numb

And that my love is all because you caused them

You will never be the one who loves me

but your cruel attempt to bury me will be
the reason my book is on that shelf

and how a little girl just like me comes across these words
and learns to let her monster go too

—You have to give credit where credit is due—

THE
Garden
IN THE
Sky

And I'll never know why

God thought he needed you back home more than I did

here on earth

I can't say I agree

or trust his decision

but here on earth my heart aches day in

and day out

because although you're in heaven

it's hell down here without you

Not a day goes by that I can't look at a picture of your face

or remember the last few memories we had together

before you left this place

Not an hour goes by that I don't hear your voice

through the radio station

Not a second passes that I don't wish you were here to see me now

Not a moment goes by that I don't miss your smile,

I'd do anything to fly up to heaven and visit you for just a little while

I wasn't old enough to understand

All I knew was that I'd miss you forever

Here I am 16 years later

Still wondering how I manage to

survive each day without you

The only thing I want in life

Is to make you proud

And I hope more than anything that I haven't let you down

Because if there is anyone in this world
I love more than my heart can bear

It is you

As I wait for the chance that my life may continue

I imagine better days

I see myself on the field again

In a car again

with my friends

my family

growing old

but we aren't all that lucky

I dream of a better tomorrow

in hopes that today will end well

that when today ends

my life does not end with it

but I won't know for sure

until I wake up tomorrow morning

but I don't sleep

I won't

I can't

continued...

...continued

Every time I close my eyes

embers burn

and so does my skin

but the worst ache of all

is in my heart

I can't seem to forget the feeling

knowing that I could lose everything

and all of those things could lose me

If I go

remember me as I was

not what I have become

I try to forget that night

the night when

I felt everything

and then I felt nothing

—*Niko Strong*—

I remember that day as if it was yesterday

It should have been yesterday

That I last saw your face

Held your hand

Heard your voice

I think I forgot the sound

I need to hear the sound

You came home from work

your clothes a mess

as a promise to see me tomorrow spilled from your lips

You sent me your love and went on your way

I spent the rest of that night counting down the

hours

minutes

seconds

until I would see you again,

but I would never see you again

I remember that day as if it was yesterday

It shouldn't have ever occurred

I remember the news I refused to believe

The tears created a tsunami in our living room

continued...

BRENNA KATSOUDAS

Only 4

and trying to hold everyone

everything

together

You slipped away from the world

and left us behind

We picked up the pieces but they shattered every single damn time

You were sunlight in the darkest room

The smile that lit up my world

You were the man I loved from the moment I breathed air

As whole as I have become

I always find a piece of myself missing

I look for it in these men

but I never realized until now

It's not them I'm missing

It's you

Hung up on my wall

the last piece of evidence that you and I existed in the same lifetime

So many years ago our two souls occupied
a charcoal couch with the comfiest of cushions

two innocent smiles who had not a clue

that one of us would be leaving many years far too soon

A pink tea cup in my hand

Multi colored jelly beans in a plastic bag

Labatt blue in a cold can, held by rough gentle hands

Someone I was lucky enough to know
for such a short amount of time

You lit up my tiny little world with your big brown eyes

I say goodnight to our picture every night before I go to sleep

No matter where I end up in this world I'll never be afraid

I know you're always with me

—θείος Χρήστος, *I feel you with me everywhere I go*—

Discovering
Gravity

I dream of dreams

in dreams

through dreams

Never asleep

but only when I am awake

for reasons I do not understand

Wasting away the night in reality

spending my days in a fantasy

Tossing my heart in the air

turning thoughts of love

into thoughts of hate

a game I learned from none other than you

Perhaps the reason I dream of dreams

in dreams through dreams

in the daylight

Exactly why I fail to do so when night falls

And in those dreams it is you and I

but never under the moonlight

always under the rays of the sun

God forbid I lay and earn a well nights rested sleep
like the rest of the human race

continued...

SUPERNOVAS OF THE HEART

But

I wasn't meant to live the life of plenty

for I was meant to experience extraordinary things

and people

Although the wounds are my price to pay

I certainly wouldn't have it any other way

I've never wanted to be anything less than red

Some of us were meant to bleed ourselves dry with the love
we give to the ones who can't find it in themselves

Some of us were built to survive the storms that rage in our hearts,

while others were born to create those storms

Some of us were left in the cold

by the ones who stole every last bit of warmth

Some of us were bruised and battered

by the ones who can't control the anger
that unleashes inside of them when jealousy arises

Some of us were meant to be pushed down to the ground

until we were pronounced dead,

but we stood up countless times

Some of us

The mighty hearts of the world

made with endless amounts of

blood

tears

and scar tissue

We will rise

time

and time

again

Once my strength was discovered,

I was unstoppable

Moving mountains with my finger tips

creating stories with my eyes

filling empty hearts

drawing colors across the sky

bringing the sun back into galaxies that spent eons in darkness

All because I was the moon

with a secret that opened up other worlds

As I breathed in new oxygen

the words came to life

the stars told me to love myself

and nothing has ever been the same since that night

BRENNA KATSOUDAS

I once wrote, "If I were to write a book I would make sure to thank you, after all you have given me all of this." How confused I must have been to allow you credit for the wondrous lines of poetry I had created in my mind from the ruins you left my heart to die in. From now on, I thank myself. After all, I would have nothing if I didn't have her.

Someday

you are going to need the love I was willing to give you

and maybe

just maybe

it won't be yours to have anymore

It's not going to happen

You're not going to find the answers to why he left

or why it hurts so bad

by scrolling through meaningless apps

no matter how hard you try

because

the real answers are only inside of his head

but soon you'll never have to worry again darling because

there will be a time when no one will be able to even find it in
themselves to leave you like this

A pure heart has been broken

time

and time

again

but never fails to keep loving

because it's all she knows how to do

Words make it easy to fool

but darling, don't fall for his miss arrangement of letters

for the lovely words he uses

do not make up his name

they're just a bunch of letters rearranged as a pretty lie

love yourself enough to let him go

—*Unscrambled lies*—

If you asked me 338 days ago if I knew what I was getting myself into

I wouldn't have had a clue as to what you were talking about

For the next 39 days I would learn exactly that

If you asked me 299 days ago what happened

I would have told you your guess was as best as mine

299 days ago

I would spend the next 139 days trying to get him to come back,
without ever exchanging words

because I knew he wouldn't reply

When I woke up 204 days ago I wasn't expecting the next 44 days to
happen the way they did

204 days ago he came back

without an explanation

without an apology

204 days ago, I let him

For the next 44 days I ate, slept and breathed him

And on the 44th day he decided that 5 days more
than the last time was too much

and vanished once more

If you asked me 160 days ago if I knew it was coming
since 44 days ago when he returned

I would have said yes

If you asked me everyday for the next 113 days if I would have
changed a thing

I would have said no

continued...

If you asked me that now, my answer would remain the same

113 days after the second disappearance I asked him why

On the 114th day he gave me his best answer

And on the 115th day I finally received the closure
I had been searching for since 257 days prior

when he first walked away

Today has been 338 days since you made your way into my life

I have survived everyday in between

From the first 139 days without you

to the 160 days after our last 44 days together

and even with the closure, i'd give anything to have you back

even just for another day

But I have lived 6,905 days

and you have only been present in my mind for 338 of those days

Which means I have lived 6,567 days without the mere thought of you

I plan on living 5 times the amount I have already achieved
whether you are a part of those days, or not

I miss you like hell

but just because you're gone, doesn't mean I have to be

and that is the answer I have been searching for

—160 days and counting—

There is a force as strong as the moon pulling the tide, pulling me back to you. And I have been trying to set myself free since the day I stepped foot inside of your prison, but each time I open the door I end up locking myself back in. And although I blame you for making me want to stay, I know in my heart that no one can make me do anything at all. In the end it has always been my decision to let the tide control me; I have risen above the moon and it's incredible strength. I have managed to walk away. Despite the fact I turn around multiple times on my way out of this box made of metal bars and concrete, this time I have locked the door from the outside. I have released myself from the pain of holding on far too long and much too tight. I understand you may be confused, but you mustn't overlook all you have put me through. It is now your turn to make your way to the door and learn how to be strong enough to unlock it and leave everything inside, only taking yourself along with the wind. Although your existence has caused discomfort towards my heart, I hope you find it in yourself to leave behind the person you have created with little white lines and thick clouds of smoke. I pray that you will begin to see everything that you could be outside of this cage.

Set yourself free.

What I thought was the biggest loss of my life

was one of my biggest lessons

What broke my heart

taught me how to heal it

The heartache attached was so wild

that watching these men come and go

no longer affects the beating life inside of my chest

for I have already experienced terrible pain

Nothing can touch me now

I'm sick of fighting with you everyday. I do everything in my power to keep my head afloat, and you are doing everything in yours to drown me. We go back and forth all day long. I wish I could escape you, but I can't because you're ALWAYS there. Wide awake or sleeping, alert or far away dreaming. You scare everyone away, you don't even give them a chance. And if I defy you, you only punish me. As unfortunate as this all is I don't think you realize what you're doing. Everyday, every fight we have, I only get stronger. I'm figuring you out. I'm winning. Every time I fight back, you lose because I refuse to give up. And one day my voice will drown out the sound of yours, and none of us will even remember you.

—A letter to the voices in my head.—

If it weren't for all of the poets and the life rafts
they drew up in pretty words

I wouldn't be here at all

at least not anymore

Going to the gym and lifting heavier weights

is not realizing your own strength

It's when you are so low there doesn't seem to be anything above

When the sun rises out the window

but the one in your soul remains black

And no one is around to light the flame

no one searches for you through the darkness

forgotten and lost within the deadly thoughts remaining in your mind

It is not until you begin to rise from the depths of your despair

the first glint of hope

each ray of sunshine

bringing your tired

aching soul

back to life

You

Reaching up and dragging yourself out of this black hole that
swallowed every last bit of hope you held on to

and taking it back

Claiming it as your own

standing above the abyss

reflecting on your past

giving yourself another reason to carry on

finding it in yourself to love yourself the way
you've always loved others

making this one count

because it is finally mutual

They say time heals all

They say you don't just wake up one day and everything is better

I spent days

weeks

months

trying to get better

praying each day

hoping the next would be different

holding on to the day when my smile would be real again

when I would feel happiness rush through my veins like a drug

Until I woke up one April morning

to all of my wishes wrapped up tightly in a box around my heart

A small tag hung off the box

I took a closer look

To: Brenna

From: God

It is proven

that in order to appreciate joy, you must suffer

Although it is an ugly thing to imagine

it is nonetheless true

In order to enjoy the sun

you must learn to dance in the rain

You came into my life and took something from me that wasn't yours

the words from my heart

and made them yours

Once upon a time I believed you were the reason for these lovely
words

but I was terribly wrong

I write because I feel, I don't write for you, I write because of you

But don't flatter yourself honey,

everything I've ever written about you came from the broken pieces,

not the whole ones

I've spent so much time trying to get better

You can't just show up

like you own the place

and then decide you've had your fun

just to leave me lonely

That's just how it goes

that's how it always goes

Darling it breaks my heart to see you believe each time

holding onto faith

bleeding love

and in return receiving nothing but emptiness

Waking up the next morning willing to try again

That is what makes you a warrior

You see

it is always worth the pain

because once it's all done

I have these breathtaking words among this paper to be proud of

that will someday heal the hearts of the ones like me

up at 4 am

searching

between endless book pages

for just one simple reason to stay

I pray that someday I can accept the kind things other people tell me and maybe even believe them. I pray that someday what others say is only ever the truth and not an ounce of a lie. I hope that one of these days peace can lie within our souls knowing that if we tried our best, that is really all we can do. And that you can not force someone to love you, no matter how much you may love them. And that people change and there is absolutely nothing we can do about it.

The point of writing these poems was to heal my heart

and learn how to let yours go

I struggled for so long, I'm sure you could tell

My heart still aches for you, but it murmurs a little quieter

and stings a little less

Although this is what I've been waiting for

guilt consumes me

as I detach the strings connecting our hearts

Truth is, It's the last thing I desire

you will always be a piece of me

but maybe someday I can only hope the longing will suffice

These words have been my medicine

while you were my vice

None of this means I have erased you from my memories

I'm just learning to live without you

isn't that what you've been teaching me to do all this time?

Isn't this what you wanted?

I am the remedy

for when you are lonely,

sad

and lost

When you feel like giving up,

I am the remedy

When you are ready to throw the towel in and end it all,

the days when you have no idea why you're here anymore

I am the remedy

The thing that gives you reassurance
that you do indeed have a purpose

For when you've dried me out and left me to starve

I am the remedy

For all of the times you damaged my soul
just so you could feel something

I've learned to heal myself

I am the remedy

Have you ever truly and wholeheartedly fallen in love with yourself?
So deeply it scares you to remember the times when you hated her?

How crazy to think

how I used to think

How crazy to not remember how it used to feel

How insane it is to know every time I thought I'd die without you,
I was given a hundred more reason to live

And now all of the sad songs I used to relate to

don't relate to me anymore

And all of the heartbreak I wrote

doesn't apply to mine anymore

And every single tear I shed

dried up a long time ago after you'd been gone

And all of my anger toward you washed away,
I swore I'd never let it see the light of day

And I was given another chance to redeem myself
of all I was, and all I am

Here I stand

mighty in my shoes

to not only show you

but the world

that I made it out of your treacherous hole of what are now lies

because my reflection remained the same

but you seem to have an awfully different face

It is with great confidence I must confess

I do not need you

You no longer have the power to make me blue

because

someone else is going to turn my blood yellow

and what's the point of waiting for you to do so

when it's what you should have been doing all along?

For I shall thank you

It is the pain you have inflicted upon my heart
that gave me these heart wrenching words

And if there ever comes a day that I love you more than the moon

you must know,

that you have my heart

And if you choose to misuse your power

I will create a tsunami more powerful
than the moons ability to pull the tide

That will be the day you fear me

Sometimes you need to have the pieces
broken in order to find the ones that belong

and the ones that never did

It was in that moment I realized

that I was dancing in the mirror

and singing in the shower

because I loved myself

Red

Blue

Purple

creases across my skin

traveling to my

Red

Blue

Purple

hips

marked with grooves between pure, clean skin

making their way to my

Red

Blue

Purple

bottom

a plump mess of dark lines

ending their journey at my

Red

Blue

Purple

thighs

holding lines of demarcation up and around

making it known

that I have indeed grown

The world seems to rotate a bit differently

when you love the soul staring back at you in the mirror

I am happy. I am content, but don't let that fool you. I still have my unbearable moments. I still have plenty of days where disappearing feels like the only option. But those days have now become the smallest fraction of my life. For the incredible moments are far more common. Yellow shines through every window, crack and crevice. And it's all because I discovered the love I had for myself hidden behind everyone who never loved me.

Maybe someday someone other than you

will see all of the light that radiates off of your skin,

all of the love you hold inside the walls of your heart

I am a bundle of sunshine

a ray of light

all things sugar, candied and spiced

I hold this planet we occupy in the palm of my hand

My face is upon every flower in all of the fields, in all of the land

Untouchable to you,

so very far out of reach

I admire my insides more than what you can see

if only you took the time to get to know this

I am something so extraordinary

how unfortunate you'll never have the chance to experience any of it

—*To every single boy who ever called me boring*—

You weren't put on this earth to be remembered by all, you were put on this earth to be appreciated by the people that deserve you. Not everyone will find you special, but the people that do will never be able to forget you.

Maybe once you realize

that you are the glue

that mends every broken heart

and searches through the cracks for every lost soul

Then you will feel how powerful your existence on this planet
is to all of the souls you touch with your precious heart

I fell in love with myself

and so I learned to fall in love with people who loved me too

When I close my eyes

I see the greenest grass,

someday it will be mine

And when I open my eyes

the grass beneath my feet begins turning the brightest shade of green

creating a look of jealousy within the eyes of the trees aside

When I look to the other side, it oddly mirrors the same

so does the young girl standing above it,

that is her side

And who am I

to determine who has the greenest grass

The shape of your face

the length of your nose

the curve in your smile

everything down to your toes

none of it matters to any degree

unless your inside is filled with art from
all the galleries in all the galaxies

None of it means a thing

unless the shape of your heart

is bigger than your ego

and the length of your patience is a long path to heaven

that leads to the curve of your wonderful existence in this world

Bringing you full circle

to make you understand

that everything on the outside means absolutely nothing

if the inside is rotted hollow

It's okay to not be able to do things on your own. Isolating yourself and putting so much weight on your shoulders just so that you can say that you've accomplished all of these things on your own is such a waste of energy. Let people in. Allow people to help you. If you push everyone away, you'll only have yourself to blame in the end. Open up your heart, and allow all the love in the world to enter it and fill you with eternal happiness. Yes, you can make yourself happy but sometimes it's okay to want someone else to do it for you.

—*You are strong regardless. Let love in.*—

She was someone I once knew, way back when

the girl somewhat like me, who knew pain as her only friend

As our legs grew longer, years added to our age

as did wisdom and a new perspective on life
and the way our friendship remained

Once we were forced apart it was the truth
that clung to the spot we once held

A heap of memories so far in the distance

reminding us that what we needed then

had now been outgrown

shedding 6 years of chicken wing dinners
and tears sprung from endless amounts of laughter

You will always be someone I choose to remember in the light of day

always managing to save me from my own falling grace

even though you hit the bottom so very long ago

—*Long live*—

I am love

in all things

You have given me so many reasons to fall in love with me

Keep yourself busy with art,

it helps heal the mind of heartbreak

—*When your inspiration is the thing that broke your heart, write.*—

I have been writing lately

and

I have come to the realization

that

you did not

spark the fire under my passion

I have come to understand

that

You

were the flame

the reason

for my self destruction

You

were the reason I could not form all of the words I had created

I couldn't even find them anymore

because

when you walked away

you packed up all of the things I loved,

but you were never good at hiding things

And now I write beautiful poems for me

because they're my favorite

—The truth unraveled after I set myself free—

All of the words pressed against my chest so viciously that if I didn't choose to write them down on my own they would rip me apart and leave me in millions of pieces laid out beneath your feet.

—Do not take these words for granted—

I heard my pulse beating a little louder than usual that night

I came to the conclusion that it was my body reminding me that although I felt broken

I was still alive

standing tall on my own terms

not willing to be torn down the middle

by the evil actions of a man who never actually knew me

If you live your life in fear of death's shadow

you will spend all of eternity stuck in the quicksand of regret

Surrounded by all of the things you were too afraid to do

while you had the gift of chance

Everyday that you woke up and carried on was meant for you

Every moment you wanted to disappear,
but didn't, made you that much stronger

Together hand in hand

we cleaned up his mess

everything he stole, we got back

everything he broke, we put back together

Partners in crime

—*Me, Myself, and I*—

My hand has laid itself upon bookshelves in all different forms

and colors

My heart has been strung along by a million different lovers

And my soul has been torn apart by every boy
who made his way inside of my pretty little head

and marked my heart with bruises and lies

using paints the color of cotton candy skies

With every bad boy came another insecurity

And a piece of me disappeared with every doubt of my worth

because the people I allowed my time, never really deserved it

It took me eons to realize the depths to the pain they caused

and the only thing that made me want to stay

were the words the men and women wrote before me

in stanzas like this

reminding me of the reasons I breathe

Singing lullabies into my delicate ears

that once only knew lies

Never failing to shine light into my soul

that was once coated in eternal darkness

How I wish I could thank you all for reminding me
how strong I've always been

when I didn't feel an ounce of strength left in me at all

—To the creators of the words that saved me—

In the midst of all the reasons you've found to leave

I promise there will always be one good one that reminds you to stay

It is much deeper than a man who hurt you. It goes down to each root that sprung from the dirt in your lovely garden. Each root that formed a poisonous flower. Some flowers were boys, some flowers were old friends and most flowers went by the name of self destruction. Cutting down the flowers never worked. But the day you rose from the dead and ripped each pretty floral stem from its root and laid everyone of them out to die, was the day you won the battle. Each day you return to the garden and plant your own flowers, showering them with love and pure sunshine. And everyday another girl learns to do the same.

It has been a long,

windy

continuous road

but we made it

You and I

A beautiful journey in which "impossibility" seemed to describe it best

With you my darling, nothing is impossible

especially when it involves love

—A letter to the heart I healed—

CLOSING LETTER FROM THE AUTHOR

I am just someone with a bundle of thoughts inside of her head. A little too much thinking and enough writing to fill every page in all of the notebooks in the world. I have been writing for quite some time and it has become one of my most favorite things to do. Many of my close friends, family and people who have taught me a few things before they had to go, have encouraged me to share my art with the world but I have been utterly shy. It is a very difficult concept to pour your heart out onto paper and then place it in the hands of someone, giving them the ability to see right through you in that very moment. I contemplated this for a long time. I finally decided that the thoughts in my head must be heard and must be shared. I have come to fall in love with my complicated brain overtime. I despised it for various reasons, but there have been a few beautiful human beings who have taught me to love every thought I put to paper because I have the power to create a feeling with only a few words. The things I chose to share with you took a great deal of bravery, but I can only hope that it will be worth it. Thank you to those who have given me the courage to do so, taking me completely out of my comfort zone to the point of many tears. I cannot thank you enough for pushing me until I (finally) gave in. I couldn't have done this without any of your kind words and the overwhelming amount of love each and everyone of you showed me. You know who you are, at least I truly hope you do.

ABOUT THE AUTHOR

Brenna Katsoudas is a full time hairdresser and freelance makeup artist from Upstate New York with a rooted love for meaningful words and books of all kinds. She spends most of her days in the salon, although her head is always up in the clouds creating poems every chance she gets. *Supernovas of the Heart* stems from her deep love for the moon and the lovely midnight sky that often keeps her company during her past midnight writing sessions. Brenna has been  writing for many years now and has always dreamed of writing a book of her own. Realizing her passion for writing very early on, she began to find poetry was her very strong point later on in life. Some of the poems she chose to include are from her much younger years that have evolved into something much more mature. She plans on continuing down her writing path to see where it is destined to take her. To keep up with her journey and possible sneak peaks of poetry in the works you can follow her on Instagram @brenna.kaitlin.

The beautiful cover and small illustrations included in my book were illustrated by the extremely talented Elizabeth Whelan.

For more of her work visit her website
elizabethwhelan.carbonmade.com
and follow her Instagram *@ewhelan_art*